Lamborghini

BY THOMAS E. BONSALL

GALLERY BOOKS
An Imprint of W. H. Smith Publishers Inc.
112 Madison Avenue
New York City 10016

Contents

ISBN 0-8317-5412-5

PREFACE

Few of the world's important automobile manufacturers have had as traumatic and sensational a history as has Lamborghini. Like Enzo Ferrari, whose famed company has, from the inception, been the chief competitor, the founder of Lamborghini, Ferruccio Lamborghini, was a man dedicated to excellence and possessed of an instinctive sense of good design. Unlike Enzo Ferrari, however, whose entire life was wrapped up in the construction, racing and development of automobiles, Lamborghini was an industrialist whose products were somewhat less spectacular. They included such seemingly mundane items as tractors, heating devices and air conditioners--all necessary to civilization but hardly the stuff of which dreams are made. Lamborghini's enterprises, however, were immensely profitable and, as a result, he could afford to indulge himself with the acquisition of exotic and expensive automobiles.

As has happened on more than one occasion throughout the history of the automobile, Lamborghini's passion could ultimately be satisfied only by the manufacture of an automobile bearing his name. One is reminded of the classic story of James Ward Packard. In the early days of the auto industry on the United States he purchased a Winton automobile. Finding it unsatisfactory, he complained personally to Alexander Winton, whose famous retort was to the effect that if Packard thought he could build a better

automobile, he should do it himself. Packard
could and did--and the world gained one of its
most illustrious automotive names as a result.
In similar fashion, the first Lamborghini 350
GT came to production in 1964 when Ferruccio
Lamborghini became convinced he, too, could
do a better job himself.

The Lamborghini should never be
thought of as if it were a mere counterpart to
the Ferrari, though. From the very beginning it
was a true alternative, possessing a personality
unlike any other high-performance automobile.
Moreover, Lamborghini soon became identified
with advanced concepts that other
manufacturers only dreamed about.
Lamborghini embraced them with open arms--
and an open mind--and converted his dreams
and visions into production reality. Yet,
Lamborghini wasn't immune to the unforgiving
dynamics of the real world of economics.
Lacking the immense financial strength of the
Ferrari organization, Lamborghini (like
Maserati and Aston Martin) eventually fell upon
hard times during the difficult years of the
seventies.

While the situation did not descend to the
level of liquidation, it did see the company
deteriorate from a position of considerable
economic strength through a tumultuous series
of owners and even receivership. This process
culminated with the purchase of Lamborghini
by Chrysler Motors in 1987. Now, with a
strong financial partner behind it, plus a world-
wide economic recovery and stabilized fuel
prices, it's more certain than ever that the
company's proven skills of innovation and
quality will continue to result in the kind of
glorious vehicles for which the name
Lamborghini has become justly famous. It is in
that perspective that this volume is presented as
a prelude to even greater glories from
Lamborghini.

frontale

Studiata nella parte anteriore per ottenere un'alta penetra-
zione all'aria per l'elevata velocità che può raggiungere,
presenta una nuova sistemazione dei fari, ora doppi e
affiancati con gli abbaglianti
all'interno e gli anabbaglianti
all'esterno, e con i fanalini
di posizione collocati sui
baffi dei paraurti realizzati
in acciaio inossidabile.
Nella parte anteriore della
carrozzeria, al limite della
fiancata e appena sotto il
parabrezza sono collocate
due prese di aria protette
da una grigliatura, che
immettono direttamente
un flusso d'aria nell'abita-
colo, assicurando un facile
e rapido ricambio ed una
perfetta ventilazione.

8

350/400

SUGGESTIVE OF GREATNESS

It has been noted that no matter how hard you pull on the neck of a duck, you won't end up with a swan. Still, more than one celebrated automobile has begun life as an ugly duckling only to end up as an automotive swan. Consider the Lamborghini. When it was first displayed at the October, 1963, Turin Auto Show, the 350 GTV seemed a hopeless mishmash of dated styling cliches, the lines of its Scaglione-designed body more often than not in serious conflict with each other. None-the-less, the 350 GTV possessed other, more impressive credentials strongly suggestive of great future potential--perhaps enough to seriously challenge Ferrari's pre-eminent position among the world's exotic cars.

The engine was an aluminum alloy , 60° V-12 with cast iron liners and fitted with four, chain-driven overhead cams. A 3.03 inch borem and 2.44 inch stroke resulted in a displacement of 211 cubic inches (3464 cc). A cast aluminum cylinder head featuring hemispherical combustion chambers was part of the package.

In all, this was an impressive beginning-- but barely more than that. By October, 1964, when the London Automobile Show opened, Lamborghini had determined the direction which he wanted to follow and the result was a vastly improved product. Touring, the coachbuilder who in the interim had been given the responsi-

bility for Lamborghini design, extensively altered the 350 GTV's excessively fussy front and rear, confused side trim and awkward rear lights and bumper. The six exhaust pipes were reduced to a more comprehensible four, while the retractable headlights gave way to oval-shaped Cibie, contributing much to the Lamborghini's increasingly distinctive appearance.

The Touring body was constructed of aluminum and mounted upon a tubular, ladder-type frame. Touring described this construction as "Superleggera." Early models by Touring had a simple mesh grille insert but later versions carried two chrome bars. There was just a hint of the Ferrari 275 GTB in the inward sweep of the fenders but, beyond that probably coincidental similarity, the two marques had little in common.

Although the 350 GT was not promoted as a 2+2, the storage area behind the front seats could, if needed, be used to accommodate two small children--or two extremely small and/or friendly adults. However it was used, this space was easily reached through the Lamborghini's unusually wide door openings. The twin leather-covered bucket seats were separated by a wide console. Instrumentation was more than complete, it was awesome.

As expected, no major revisions were made at this time in the V-12 Lamborghini engine. With side draft 40DCOE Webers and a 9.5:1 compression ratio, the 350 GT engine was rated at 336 hp at 6500 rpm. Torque was rated at 254 lb-ft at 5700 rpm. A ZF, five-speed all-syncromesh transmission was fitted.

Beneath this skin was a modern, all-independent suspension. A limited-slip differential was standard. Wheelbase was 96.5 inches, length was a trim 177 inches.

The performance of the 350 GT was, as expected, exceptional. Its handling exhibited few vices. A top speed approaching 155 mph combined with a 0-60 mph time of under seven seconds placed the 350 GT well within the realm of Ferrari's Grand Touring models.

Output of the 350 GT, which listed in the United States for $13,900, was limited to just 131 units from 1964 to the cessation of production in 1967.

The rapid pace of evolution at Lamborghini was typified by the arrival of the 400 GT 2+2 in early March, 1966. This model was easily differentiated from the 350 GT by its dual headlights and considerably smaller rear window, but Lamborghini watchers could also detect its higher roofline, and more sharply raked windshield and backlight. Not as readily apparent were the all-new exterior body panels or the longer, 100.3 inch wheelbase.

Since production of the 400 GT 2+2 was expected to substantially exceed that of the 350 GT, a switch from aluminum to steel body construction was made, resulting in a slight increase in curb weight to 2,734 pounds. With the exception of larger trunk capacity, creature comforts remained essentially as before.

A larger, 3.23 inch bore increased the V-12's displacement to 239.7 cubic inches (3929 cc), contributing to a rise in horsepower to 320 (DIN at 6500 rpm). Maximum torque now stood at 276 ft-lb (at 4500 rpm).

A point of justifiable pride for Ferruccio Lamborghini was the 400's new Lamborghini-designed-and-built five-speed, all-synchromesh transmission and differential, which replaced units purchased from ZF and Salisbury, respectively.

During its production run from 1966 to 1968, a total of 224 examples of the 400 GT 2+2 were built. The four liter engine was also available in a two-seater body as the 400 GT. Twenty-three of these latter coupes versions were constructed--three with aluminum bodies, the remainder with steel bodywork. In the United States, the 400 GT 2+2's price (in 1968) of $14,750 was more than competitive with corresponding models from Aston Martin, Ferrari and Maserati.

BORGHINI 400 GT 2+2

Miura
THE FIRST TOUR DE FORCE

A mere three years after its inception, Automobili Ferruccio Lamborghini SpA stunned the automotive world with the Lamborghini Miura. This automobile was, from virtually every point of view, a tour de force.

Development of the Miura began in late 1964. Approximately one year later, in November, 1965, a Miura chassis was displayed at the Turin Salon. The motoring world had its first look at the Miura's sensational styling at the March, 1966, Geneva show. By the time of the October, 1966, Paris Salon, the Miura had changed substantially from its initial form.

The placement of a V-12 engine transversely behind the passengers posed major noise and heat problems, so the Miura's designers soon abandoned the sloping rear window of the prototype for a series of slats through which engine heat and noise were allowed to exit. To adequately insulate the Miura's occupants from both uncomfortable heat and sound levels, a double-thickness, vertically positioned "Visarm" plexiglass window was positioned directly in front of the engine. In addition, a four inch layer of polystyrene was installed on an aluminum bulkhead between the engine and interior.

These refinements were essential to the Miura's commercial success, of course, but the first ingredient in its recipe for modern classic status was its stunning styling. The talent behind this creation was Marcello Gandini, then in the employ of Nuccio Bertone.

With a height of a mere 41.5 inches and an overall length of 171.5 inches, the Miura's all-steel body flowed from front to rear in a series of voluptuous curves accentuated by several well-integrated grilles and vents. At the front a very wide and very low grille opening carried the directional signals and twin driving lights. Instead of the expected concealed headlights, the Miura was fitted with exposed Carello headlamps that blended into the front fender line when not in use. Surrounding the lights was a gridwork that directed air to the front brakes. Placed across the hood close to its leading edge were twin grilles that released hot air from the radiator. The right side unit also opened to provide access to the fuel filler cap.

The Miura's windshield was sharply sloped and the rear view was dominated by the back window's venetian blinds. Just the slightest hint of a spoiler was found on the upper end of the tail section surrounding the

taillights. External identification was limited to Miura script on the rear deck, a Lamborghini emblem on the hood and a Bertone logo positioned just behind the doors.

Beneath this elegant form was a platform frame. The suspension system of steel pressing wishbones and coil springs with concentric Armstrong shock absorbers was adapted from the front-engined 350 GT, 400 GT and 400 GT 2+2 models.

The Miura rode on Campagnolo 15x7 magnesium alloy knock-off wheels with five large cooling scoops. GR70VR-15 Pirelli Cinturato HS tires rated for continuous operation at 165 mph joined the package to the road.

The heart and soul of the Miura was, of course, its magnificent 3929 cc V-12 engine.

Other than its mounting position it was in most details similar to that of earlier models. Even seasoned Lamborghini enthusiasts were taken aback by the single aluminum casting for the Miura's engine block, crankcase, transmission and differential.

The Miura V-12 was rated at 350 hp. Also available was a "Sprint" version rated at 430 hp. This claimed output was always suspect, but there is little doubt it was capable of a true output approaching 400 hp. Both versions were equipped with six vertically mounted Weber 461DA3C, three-barrel carburetors. A single plate Borg & Beck clutch transferred power through the Lamborghini-built, five-speed all-synchromesh gearbox to a ZF limited slip differential.

Although no independent road test ever

reached the 198 mph maximum claimed by the factory for the Sprint-engined Miura, there is ample evidence that it was one of the fastest road cars then available. The "Motor" (August, 1970) recorded a 171 mph top speed--a figure which needs no apologies. When production ceased in 1975, a total of 900 Miuras had been built, no mean achievement for a car that, in 1967, retailed for $19,250.

Lamborghini unveiled still more powerful and refined versions of the Miura in both 1969 and 1971. The first of these, the Miura S, carried "Miura S" identification script on the right side of its rear deck. With reshaped combustion chambers, four Weber 40IDL-3L carburetors, higher-lift cams and improved breathing, the Miura S V-12 developed 370 (net) hp at 7700 rpm. Maximum torque was 286 lb-ft at 5000 rpm. The foregoing changes enabled the Miura S to reach a maximum speed of between 168 and 170 mph.

In addition, a rerouted exhaust system permitted a modest increase in luggage space. Higher quality materials were used for the Miura's vinyl seats and carpeting and electric window lifts were included in the Miura S's $19,250 price.

The Miura SV--"Super Veloce"--was introduced at the 1971 Geneva Show. It was distinguished by its nine-inch wheels, Pirelli Cinturato, FR70VR-15 low-profile tires, larger rear wheel cut outs and chrome door handles. With a higher, 10.7:1, compression ratio, its maximum horsepower rating was boosted to 385 at 7850 rpm.

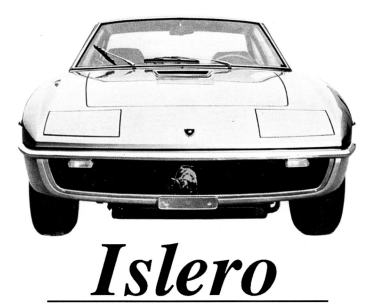

Islero
THE END OF THE BEGINNING

Produced in far fewer numbers than the Espada, which was introduced almost concurrently, the Islero represented the final form of Lamborghini's original front-engined grand touring concept. Mechanically, it was virtually identical to the 400 GT 2+2, but larger front and rear anti-roll bars were fitted and the overall length was five inches shorter than that of the 400 GT.

Providing the Islero with an important performance edge over the older model was its lighter weight. Approximately 240 pounds were trimmed. Road test results indicated a top speed of an outstanding 161 mph. A limited-

slip differential was standard, as were 11.8 inch front and 11.0 inch rear disc brakes. Pirelli Cinturato G70VR15 tires were mounted on seven inch Campagnolo knock-off, alloy wheels.

The interior arrangement of early Islero models placed most gauges in a readable, if somewhat haphazard, arrangement. Later versions were far neater with the large tachometer and speedometer, which were separated by an oil temperature gauge, placed directly before the driver. The remaining five gauges (fuel, ammeter, oil pressure, water temperature and clock) were lined up in the

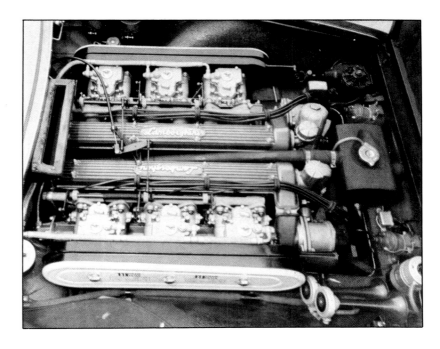

same dash cove. Superseding the Islero's original push-pull switches were safer, rocker types. Also abandoned in favor of a simpler, two spoke wood-rimmed steering was the original three spoke model. The passenger's dash bar was no longer installed. An elegant center console with Islero identification was a key feature of the Islero's interior redesign.

The styling of the Islero represented a sharp departure from the 400 GT's highly original and controversial design. The Islero's more conservative styling was done by Marazzi, who had picked up 400 GT 2+2 production after the demise of Touring. Only a wide chrome rocker panel bar and the wrap-around edges of the Islero's high-mounted front and rear bumpers graced its profile. Retractable headlights, a simple, center-positioned hood-scoop and a straight forward grille housing supplementary road lights gave the Islero a marked similarity to the contemporary Maserati. Still, a very large rear window, aggressive fender lines and a distinctive rear end featuring rectangular taillights placed beneath the two-piece bumper gave the Islero an overall look unshared by its peers.

Production of the $20,000 Islero spanned the years from 1967 to 1970. A total of 225 were built, including a number of Islero S versions with more powerful, 350 hp engines, up 30 hp from the standard version.

Espada

150 MPH WITH STYLE

When the forerunner of the Espada--the 2-liter Marzal--first appeared at the 1967 Geneva Salon, both Lamborghini and Bertone insisted it was not a production prototype. The controversy surrounding this car's transparent, gullwing doors and unusual honeycombed rear window overshadowed the advancement in the design of high-performance, luxury four-seater automobiles it represented. When the Espada entered into production in 1968, however, its importance as a 150 mph luxury four-seater was quickly understood.

Unlike the Marzal, whose six-cylinder engine was positioned mid-ship, the front-engined Espada was powered by Lamborghini's 3929 cc V-12. This engine was rated at 320 DIN hp at 4500 rpm. Carburetion was by six 40DCOE, two-barrel Webers and a 9.5:1 compression ratio was claimed.

In 1969, the introduction of the Series II Espada was highlighted by the use of the 350 hp Islero S engine as its standard power plant. Both engines, as well as the Espada's five-speed transmission and the ZF limited-slip differential, were virtual twins to those used in the Islero. Since the Espada was a luxury sports car, its all-independent suspension was fitted with softer springs and shock absorbers than the Islero. Smaller anti-roll bars were also installed.

A wheelbase of 104.3 inches and an overall length of 185.8 inches made the Espada the longest Lamborghini yet offered to the public. Overall height was 46.4 inches and the Espada's width was 71.2 inches. Thus by way

of comparison to the older 400 GT 2+2, the Espada was 3 inches wider and 4 inches lower. This permitted an interior fitted with four seats and ample leg and luggage room. The rear seats were identical to those in front except for the absence of adjustable back rests.

Early production models were fitted with an interior dominated by an amazing array of geometric shapes, few of which were circular. Most of the angles of the older version were removed from the Series III interior. The Series III Espada, introduced in 1973, had a revised dash panel which placed all instrumentation in a curved cove behind the steering wheel. Secondary switches were placed on the console. Also offered, beginning in 1973, was Chrysler's three-speed Torqueflite automatic transmission.

Even after production of the Espada--
which totalled nearly 900 cars--ceased in 1978,
its styling was far from dated. Its low profile
featured large side windows providing both
excellent interior vision and a light, airy
appearance. Small interior exhaust vents were
installed on the rear quarter panel while
unobtrusive, narrow vents for engine heat were
blended into a mid-bodyline crease. Twin
NACA hood ducts served to direct air to the
carburetors. Dual headlights were installed in
the outer section of the grille opening which on
the later models was covered by a black grille
mesh. The rear view of the Espada featured a
unique, two-level window arrangement. A
slatted, vertical window was installed directly
beneath the nearly horizontal hatchback
window.

Jalpa 3500

AL FRESCO REVISITED

A revamped Silhouette, called the Jalpa TP350S, was intrtoduced at Geneva in 1981. Small styling refinements, such as a reshaped B-pillar and magnesium wheels with a turbine-wheel design, gave the Jalpa visual identity. The primary distinction between the two models, however, was the Jalpa's larger engine. Its mid-ship V-8 displaced 3488 cc (213 cubic inches) and developed 250 hp at 7000 rpm. Overhead cams for each cylinder bank were featured and peak torque was 235 ft-lb at 3250 rpm. The Jalpa shared its suspension system with the Silhouette and the Urraco. Its Pirelli P7 tires measured 205/55VR-16 (front) and 225/50VR-16 (rear). These tires were mounted on 16x7 1/2 inch Campagnolo wheels.

Included in the Jalpa's list price approximately $58,000 were leather upholstery, air conditioning, AM/FM stereo-cassette, electric window lifts and an electrically-controlled mirror on the driver's side. As had been the case with the Silhouette, the Jalpa's Targa top was stowed vertically behind the seats when not in use. The collapsible spare tire was stored in the front hood compartment and 8 cubic feet of luggage space was available in the rear trunk behind the engine. At the present time the Jalpa remains in production.

Urraco

GOOD THINGS AND SMALL PACKAGES

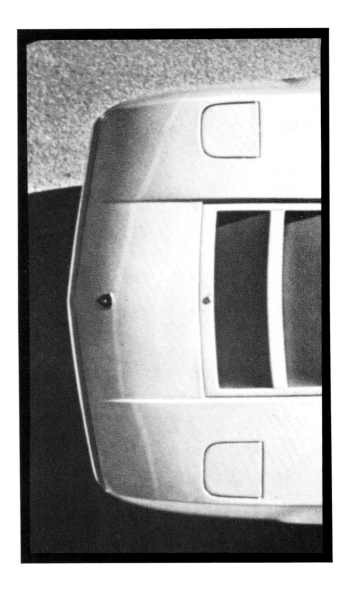

In terms of physical size, price and performance, the Urraco occupied a level a notch or two below the V-12 Lamborghini models. This segment of the market was hotly contested by Ferrari with its Dino 308 GT4 and by the Maserati Merak.

The P250 Urraco was introduced at the 1970 Turin auto show and, although it didn't actually enter into production until 1973, its Bertone styling remained exciting and contemporary. In profile, the Urraco's front end had a bullet-like form as the hood and lower fender lines converged at the junction of the long and narrow grille opening. An extremely graceful and delicate chrome bumper surrounded the upper grille line and embraced the dual running lights on European models. The more rigorous U.S. market regulations required installation of a larger, black-finish bumper. To provide reasonable, if not spacious, accommodations for the Urraco's rear seat occupants, its roofline ran nearly the body's full length. Simple rectangular taillights (two on each side), quadruple exhausts (also two on each side) and thin bumper strips provided a subdued backdrop for the Urraco's slatted rear window. Distinctive, black engine intake louvers on the rear quarter panels gave the Urraco virtually instant recognition.

Translated into English, Urraco meant "Little Bull," a term which aptly described its transversely-mounted, mid-ship V-8 engine. Constructed totally of aluminum (with the exception of steel cylinder liners), this twin-overhead-cam engine weighed just 375 pounds without manifolds but equipped with all accessories. With a bore and stroke of 3.39 inches and 2.09 inches, respectively, total displacement was 150 cubic (2463 cc).

Horsepower and torque ratings were 220 hp at 7500 rpm and 166 ft-lb at 5750 rpm, respectively. Four Weber 40IDF-1 carburetors--vertically mounted--were fitted. A 4.25:1 rear axle was standard.

The Urraco's monocoque body was based upon a sheet-steel platform. A sub-frame carried the engine, transmission and rear suspension. The P250 was mounted on a 96.5 inch wheelbase and had an overall length of 167.3 inches, a width of 69.3 inches and was 43.9 inches in height. A front trunk provided space for the spare tire, tools and air conditioning unit. Behind the engine was a second, 5.6 cubic foot trunk.

The P250's 1975 U.S. sticker price of $22,500 included the following standard equipment: air conditioning, electric windows, tinted glass, leather upholstery and an AM/FM radio. A total of 350 P250s were ultimately built.

The P111 version was produced especially for the U.S. market. It had a smaller, 1994 cc displacement by virtue of a reduced bore and used Weber 40DCNF carburetors. Its maximum horsepower was rated at 182 at 7800 rpm, with peak torque rated at 131 lb-ft at 5750 rpm. A 4.0:1 rear axle was specified. Approximately 80 examples of this version were built.

The P300 Urraco had a 3 liter engine (86 mm bore, 64.5 mm stroke), the same Weber carburetors as the P200 and a 250 hp rating at 7800 rpm. Maximum torque was 195 lb-ft at 5750 rpm. The location of its headlights was placed further forward. With a top speed in excess of 160 mph and a zero to 60 mph time in the neighborhood of 6.5 seconds, the P300 was the most potent example of the Urraco built.

After a production run of just over 600 cars, the Urraco was phased out during 1977.

Silhouette

PERFORMANCE AL FRESCO

By virtue of its removable fiberglass roof panels, the Silhouette qualified as the first open Lamborghini to enter production. A derivative of the P300 Urraco, it was introduced at the 1976 Geneva Salon and had a short and limited production run. Through 1977 only 52 were manufactured.

A side from its Targa roof, the

Silhouette's appearance differed from that of the Urraco in many ways. There were no rear quarter panel windows and in place of the Urraco's rounded wheel wells the Silhouette featured flared, squared openings for the tires. In addition, a front spoiler with inset lights, an engine oil cooler and air scoops for the front brakes were installed. For this new model, Campagnolo provided sensational magnesium wheels with a unique "five-cylinder" design. At the front, these wheels measured 15x8 inches, with 15x11 inch versions installed at the rear. Sizes for the Silhouette's Pirelli P7 tires were 195/50VR-15 (front) and 285/40VR-15 (rear), respectively. A limited use, Michelin 105X-18X tire mounted on a narrow wheel was fitted under the small front hood opening.

With the exception of stiffer springs and shocks and heavier anti-roll bars, the Silhouette suspension was identical to that of the Urraco, consisting of MacPherson struts,

lower A-arms, compliance struts, coil springs, tube shocks and an anti-roll bar. Rack and pinion steering with four turns lock to lock was installed. Vertical, 10.9 inch disc brakes with vacuum assist were used at all four wheels.

Key dimensions of the steel unit body-frame Silhouette were: 96.5 inch wheelbase, front and rear track of 58.3 inches and 60.5 inches, respectively, an overall length of 173.2 inches and a height of 43.9 inches. Compared to the Urraco, the Silhouette was 4.7 inches longer and 2 inches lower. With a displacement of 2996 cc (183 cubic inches) and a 10.0:1 compression ratio, the Silhouette's dohc V-8 developed 260 (DIN) hp at 7500 rpm. Its maximum torque of 208 ft-lb was developed at

3500 rpm. A five-speed manual transmission was standard, as was a 4.00:1 rear axle ratio.

The widely scattered instrumentation arrangement of the Urraco was supplanted with a higher-positioned Silhouette panel cluster with all gauges gathered closely together. Superseding the Urraco's shelf-mounted rocker switches were toggle switches placed on a center panel.

Countach
THE ESSENCE OF SPEED

"The first practical futuristic car."

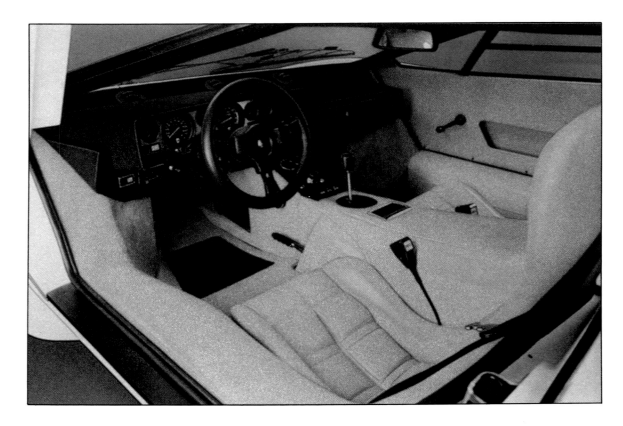

With the development of the Countach, Lamborghini not only redefined the concept of the exotic car but advanced it to a point that remains difficult to surpass even after the passage of nearly two decades. In the Lamborghini scheme of things, the Countach was the successor to the Miura, but in virtually every element of its design the Countach was a state of the art enthusiast's car, operating at the outer limits of performance and technology. The Countach was a machine intended not to pamper its occupants but to enable the driver to experience performance unequalled by any other production automobile in the world. Based on that criteria the Countach was--and remains--the best car in the world.

The Countach first appeared in March, 1971, at the Geneva show as a joint Lamborghini-Bertone idea car. Two years later, also at Geneva, it debuted as a production automobile. Styling of the Countach, by the Bertone designer, Gardini, reflected the primacy of performance in its development. In essence, Gandini was forming the outer skin of a projectile within which mechanical components were given preferential treatment over accommodations for the driver and passenger. The resulting wedge-shaped body was angular, rather than curved, and literally bristled with vents, scoops and intakes. A strangely curved rear wheel opening and vertically swinging, gas- supported doors only heightened the impact of this avant-

garde auto design. A huge NACA side scoop, together with a pair of vents on the rear deck, cooled twin vertically-mounted radiators that resided in the rear fenders. Supplying air to the engine were two large scoops just off the cockpit. Nestled between these functional units in a small indentation whose surface was rippled by another series of engine heat extracting vents was the Countach's very small and narrow rear window. The overall impression of the Countach's rear deck was that of a triumph of engineering over styling. Virtually the only concessions to conventional styling concepts were the triple rear lights (tail, stop and back-up) on either side and--for those with keen eyesight and quick reflexes who weren't sure what had just blasted past--Lamborghini Countach script.

The non-stressed external body components constructed of ultra-thin (1.0 mm) aluminum were riveted to a tubular frame. Some of the inner body panels were fabricated from an exotic "Avional" superlight alloy. The frame, with its multitude of units, suggested that of the early-sixties Maserati type 60 and 61 sports cars, but of greater importance was the safety value provided the Countach's occupants, who were effectively sheltered by a strong roll cage.

The Countach's front suspension consisted of unequal-length A-arms, coil springs and shocks with an anti-roll bar placed behind the

"The world's fastest, most beautiful and desirable production car"

The primacy of performance

T H E D

REAM

suspension components. At the rear, a single, transverse upper link, lower A-arms and twin radius rods were installed. All shock absorbers, including the two per back wheel, were expensive, lightweight Koni units with aluminum cylinder bodies and adjustments for both ride height and stiffness. No rubber bushings were used in the suspension system. Nylon elements were utilized instead. Girling 18/4, 4-piston, 10.5 inch disc brakes with ventilated alloy calipers were located at all four wheels--their first use on a production automobile. Both the Countach's rack and pinion steering (3.1 turns lock to lock) and five-speed transmission were Lamborghini designed and built. The limited slip differential was supplied by ZF and the standard rear axle ratio was 4.0:1. Respective dimensions of the front and rear Campagnolo wheels were 14x7.5 and 14x9 inches. Corresponding sizes of the standard Michelin XWX tires were 205/70-VR14 and 215/70-VR14.

The target weight for the Countach had been 2,205 pounds. At 2,390 pounds the production version came close. Contributing to this achievement was the extensive use of magnesium castings for a large number of Countach components. A partial list of these included: front and rear hub carriers, steering housing, sump, oil pump and oil filter housing, hand brake calipers, wheels and housings for gearbox and clutch.

The prototype Countach had been powered by a 4971 cc (303 cid) version of the engine was regarded as a bit too fragile for the production version, though, which was released with the V-12 in 3929 cc displacement (240 cid) form with a 3.22 inch bore and 2.40 inch stroke. Six horizontal Weber 45 DCOE, two-barrel carburetors were fitted and ratings of 375 (DIN) hp at 8000 rpm and 268 lb-ft of torque at 5500 rpm were quoted.

Unlike the transverse-position of the Miura's V-12, the Countach's engine was placed in a longitudinal location. However the nose of the engine was at the rear end of the car! Thus, the transmission (which was directly behind the cockpit) was connected to an enclosed shaft which ran alongside the engine back to the differential which was housed within the engine's oil sump casting.

In comparison to the Countach's sensational, functional styling and advanced engineering, its interior appeared conservative and subdued. A thick, three-spoke steering wheel faced a thin panel in which were installed eight Stewart-Warner gauges. Along with a 320 Km/Hr speedometer and 9000 rpm tachometer were found dials for oil pressure and temperature, coolant temperature, ammeter, voltmeter and fuel level. In addition, eight warning lights monitored such systems and functions as brakes, hand brake, alternator, air conditioning fan and compressor, parking lights, seat

Literally bristling with vents, scoops and air intakes.

Aztec architecture; 400 hp.

belts, hazard lights, high beams and directionals. A good deal of suede was used for the interior appointments and the center console both supported additional switches and provided a sturdy base for the Lamborghini's husky shifter. The two leather finished seats were of the appropriate space-age form.

From its inception, the Countach underwent an almost constant state of evolution. The first major change in its design came in 1977 with the introduction of the LP400S version. Even so, the basic format of the Countach interior remained essentially the same, although appointments were generally of a higher caliber and there was more extensive use of leather.

Larger and wider Campagnolo cast alloy wheels were installed. These measured 15x8.5 inches (front) and 15x 12 inches (rear). Also new were Pirelli P7 tires (205/50VR-15, front, and 345/35VR-15, rear). These new wheels and tires required the addition of fiberglass wheel flares. Those at the front blended into a chin spoiler while the rear versions wrapped around the back deck to terminate between the rear lights. Aside from its wheel-well flares, the S version was easily identified by its additional driving lights set low in the bumper which also was fitted with small grilles on its outer panels.

Other technical changes included the installation of 11 inch diameter disc brakes and a restructuring of the suspension geometry. The LP400S engine ratings were 353 (DIN) hp at 9500 rpm and 267 lb-ft at 5500 rpm.

The LP500S was a virtual twin to the 400S but its engine, displacing 4754 cc, was credited with 400 (DIN) hp at 7000 rpm. Peak torque output was 303 ft-lb at 4500 rpm.

Sales of the Countach in the United States required compliance with safety and emission regulations which often pushed its price into the vicinity of $85,000. Output of the LP400 was approximately 300 units through 1984.Then, in the mid-eighties, Lamborghini fell on hard economic times that finally resulted in a partial buy-in by Chrysler Motors. Thus fortified financially, Lamborghini began to plan for future models.

As this book is written the Countach remains in production, with a "super" Countach prototype being tested. The 1988 production version of the Countach uses a 5.2 liter V-12, but is otherwise similar to earlier models. The ill-conceived American "gas guzzler" tax, enacted at the height of the fuel scare years in the late-seventies, has added $3,850 to the current base sticker price of $129,000, making for a total out-the-door price of $134,850 (including $2,000 for typical destination charges and dealer prep). A rear wing is listed as a $4,000 option.

Portofino

THE SHAPE OF THINGS TO COME

The exciting Portofino is the first fruit of the Chrysler-Lamborghini union and a possible prototype for the next generation of Lamborghinis. It is instructive to remember how many of the unforgettable Lamborghinis of years past got their start as show cars.

Technically a Chrysler concept car powered by Lamborghini, the Portofino, is a unique advanced concept vehicle that was officially unveiled by Chrysler at the Frankfurt Auto Show in the latter part of 1987. The Portofino was created by Chrysler Motors' international design team. Drawing upon the expertise of Coggiola of Turin, Italy and Lamborghini, the prototype combines advanced aerodynamic styling and body design concepts with the performance of an ultimate European touring sedan. It was built by Turinese craftsmen in a remarkably short period of time.

The clean, functional styling features four rotational doors and clam-shell opening hood and decklid. The front doors pivot up and out of the way to allow for ease of entry. Ease of entry is further enhanced for rear passengers by the unibody design that eliminates the traditional "B" pillar.

The Portofino's interior has an ergonomically adjustable driver's cockpit featuring a fully adjustable instrument pod, steeing wheel and switch gear. Individual control areas are provided for all four occupants. The car's interior features hand-sewn leather. Ample luggage space is provided in both front and rear compartments.

The Portofino's engine and powertrain are pure Lamborghini. The engine is Lamborghini's 3485 cc V-8, in a mid-engine

configuration. The touring sedan offers true
sports car performance with a quoted top speed
in excess of 150 mph (240 km/h). The engine
is teamed with an all alloy Lamborghini 5-
speed transmission. Independent front and rear
suspension, with McPherson struts, coil
springs and telescopic shock absorbers
combines with ventilated disc brakes front and
rear to complete the exciting package.

Portofino Specifications

ENGINE

Mid-mounted,	90 degree V-8
	3485 cc displacement
Horsepower:	225 bhp @ 7000 RPM
Torque:	229 lb.ft. @ 3500 RPM
Bore & Stroke:	86 x 75mm

Dual overhead camshaft-chain drive
Two valves per cylinder
9.2:1 compression Ratio
All alloy construction
Wet sump lubrication
Bendix electric fuel pump

Four Weber 42 DCNF carburetors

TRANSMISSION
Lamborghini 5-speed
All alloy construction
Dry single plate clutch

BODY
Steel unibody construction
Four rotational doors
Four passenger

BRAKES
Four wheel ventilated discs

SUSPENSION
Independent front & rear
McPherson strut
Coil springs
Telescopic shocks

Acknowledgements

WRITTEN BY ROBERT C. ACKERSON & THOMAS E. BONSALL

EDITED BY THOMAS E. BONSALL
GRAPHIC DESIGN BY JUDY CRAVEN-MADISON
GRAPHIC PRODUCTION BY HAHN GRAPHICS

*THE PUBLISHERS...would like to extend their special thanks
to Chrysler Corporation and to Z. Taylor Vinson
from whose files came most of the Lamborghini material
reproduced in this book. They have been of invaluable assistance
and their unfailing cooperation in the face of deadline pressures
and other various and sundry recurring horrors of the publishing trade
has been much appreciated.*